Pursuit
and other poems

romantic extremes

DAVID J. MURRAY

iUniverse, Inc.
Bloomington

Pursuit and Other Poems
Romantic Extremes

Copyright © 2011 by David J. Murray

All rights reserved. No part of this book may be used or reproduced by any means, graphic, electronic, or mechanical, including photocopying, recording, taping or by any information storage retrieval system without the written permission of the publisher except in the case of brief quotations embodied in critical articles and reviews.

iUniverse books may be ordered through booksellers or by contacting:

iUniverse
1663 Liberty Drive
Bloomington, IN 47403
www.iuniverse.com
1-800-Authors (1-800-288-4677)

Because of the dynamic nature of the Internet, any web addresses or links contained in this book may have changed since publication and may no longer be valid. The views expressed in this work are solely those of the author and do not necessarily reflect the views of the publisher, and the publisher hereby disclaims any responsibility for them.

Any people depicted in stock imagery provided by Thinkstock are models, and such images are being used for illustrative purposes only.

Certain stock imagery © Thinkstock.

ISBN: 978-1-4620-1405-7 (sc)
ISBN: 978-1-4620-1404-0 (dj)
ISBN: 978-1-4620-1403-3 (ebk)

Library of Congress Control Number: 2011906665

Printed in the United States of America

iUniverse rev. date: 06/10/2011

Contents

Introduction 1
Ode on Emerging from an Overdose 5
Pursuit 17

August
Morningscape: 5 a.m. 20
Morningscape: The Moon Is Real 21
Morningscape: August 22
Morningscape: Vista 23
Morningscape: Wakening 24

September
Glow. 26
Too Near 27
Quiet Comes the Sun 28
Artspeak 29
My Apartment 30
Transcendence 31
Corridors 32
You, Seated 33
Venture 34
Longing 35
Colours 36
Closeness 37
Cross Grain 38
Requiredness 39

October
Hopes 42
Strand in Distance 43
A Trick of the Light 44
For Every Moment 45
Wind-Stop 46
Wind-Moment 47
Wind-Breath 48

Wind-Howl 49
Dress Code. 50
Notspeak 51
Thinking of You 52

November
Leaves. 54
Heart-Clutch 55
How Do I Feel?. 56
Diamond 57
Surprises. 58
Hiatus. 59
Softness. 60
I Have No Appetite 61

December
Holiday 64
Nearness. 65

January
Panorama 68
Winterscape 69
Onslaught. 70
From Room to Room 71
Zoo in January 72
Portrayals 73
"If" Revisited 74

February
Another Revisitation. 76
Your Voice 77
More on Your Voice .78
Monolith 79
February. 80
Greetings 81
Resting Place. 82
My Calendar. 83
Besotted 84

March
White Was the Light........................86
Your Dress................................87
Homage to *Swan Lake*.....................88
Dancing for You...........................89
No Place Out There........................90
A Slight, Immaculate Touch................91
A Special Gift............................92
How Lightly the Light Sits 93
Responses to You..........................94
Unheralded................................95
Desisting.................................96
Dating....................................97
Differential Threshold....................98

April
Animal...................................100
I Cannot Charm Thee......................101
On and On................................102
Words....................................103
Mental...................................104
Verbal...................................105
What I'll Give...........................106
What I Want..............................107
Springtime's Breath......................108
Wonderful................................109
Oh God, It's Only Saturday...............110
Eventually...............................111
Grammar Lesson...........................112

May
When the Fog Lifts.......................114
Your Presence............................115
The Barrier..............................116
Night Begins.............................117
A Generative Mind........................118
Reading..................................119
Treetops.................................120
Each Night that Dawns....................121

Blossoms. 122
Fireworks, Again. 123
Your Hair 124
Fires of Artifice. 125

June
Her Arms 128
I Don't Understand Myself .129
Wanting 130
The Miracle of Life 131
Resistance Level?. 132
Spontaneous Generation. 133

July
Fireworks Yet Again 136
Download. 137
I'll Want to Know. 138
Relief 139
You. 140

August
Shoreline. 142
The Streamline 143
The Hours Fall By. 144

September
How Late the Dawn Is 146
The Marvelous and Mystical and Magical 147

October
Portrait. 150
It Is You 151
Fade Out 152

Introduction

This volume of poetry, my sixth, is in two parts. The first part is a single long poem that was written much earlier in my life, during the dying phases of a relationship that had gone wrong. The second part is a collection of poems written during the course of a different relationship that took place at a much later time. But the two parts have something important in common; both represent the thoughts of somebody caught in "extreme" situations of the kind that can arise all too easily in the course of heterosexual human romance.

In the long poem that starts the volume, the author describes what it felt like to have made a suicide attempt, an "extreme" act that many people cannot even imagine trying to carry out. The relationship that sparked it had degenerated into a long-distance affair conducted mainly by telephone. One evening I was sitting alone in my room, drowning my frustrations in a bottle of vodka. At the bottom of the bottle, when life, like the bottle, seemed decidedly empty rather than full, an incident prompted me suddenly, in a state of alcohol-fueled incapacity, to swallow all the sodium amytal pills that I had been prescribed in order to alleviate the emotional stress that weighed on me. Some friends had been alerted to my state of mind, and it was through their intervention that the authorities entered my residence and found me comatose. I was taken to hospital where I was successfully treated. The poem begins at the point where I wake up in the recovery room of a local hospital. What the poem doesn't say was that, among the first thoughts to enter my waking brain, was a sentence to the effect that, since I was still alive, I must have "failed again."

The title of the set of 114 short poems that constitutes the second part of the book is simply *Pursuit*. No other title will do. I have not even tried to put a gloss of rationality or of moderation onto the fact that I unexpectedly met somebody to whom I was so instantly, and intensely, attracted that the only explanation was that I must have experienced "love at first sight." So I pursued her. Among the modes I adopted for the pursuit was to hide my fervor and longing behind a set of subdued and carefully crafted poems, poems so controlled that the sophisticated reader will be tempted to call the whole set an example of a Freudian defense mechanism taken to such extremes as to verge on the forbidding.

The poems are here presented in an order very close to the times at which they were written, but they are also organized in a manner that reflects the season of the year at those times. A common conceit in poetry is the "pathetic fallacy," according to which one thinks of Nature as acting in concert, so to speak, with one's own feelings. Here is a poem I once wrote, expressing that sentiment:

> This leaf is a splinter
> Of Time caught in falling,
> And heralds me winter
> And rain-clouds rolling—
> I know the rain
> Can feel my pain,
> And you, my leaf,
> My grief!

These lines illustrate the surprisingly spontaneous tendency of the poetic mind to align itself with Nature. It is an easy style to parody; yet surely thoughts like these were exactly what motivated our ancestors to invest natural objects with feelings and emotions, and, in turn, to transmute those objects into supernatural objects worthy of fear or worship.

The poems in *Pursuit* exhibit the pathetic fallacy only on occasion. In these verses, Nature and scenery and weather serve more as backdrops against which a drama is played out. Some of the most optimistic poems are written against a bitterly cold winter background, and some of the saddest poems show up against a budding and blossoming springtime. Many of the poems start with a description of a view, or an arrangement of colours on sky and lake, and move from there to something more inward. I am not imposing my feelings on Nature; Nature is imposing its presence on me.

As signposts to this background I have divided the poems into fifteen sections, each named after the month during which most of the poems in that section were written. The first section was written in August, the second in September, and so on until the October of the following year. The number of poems in each section is variable, an indication that, at the time each poem was written, I had no idea I would find myself collating them in this manner. In fact, if I *had* thought of organizing the poems with reference to the months, I would probably have tried to write the same number of poems every month out of a misguided desire to make everything neat and tidy. But nothing in the world is less neat and tidy than what one feels in the grip of an inordinate, but wholly Natural, infatuation.

I would like to thank the editorial and design teams of iUniverse for all the skill and help they devoted to producing the present volume. I also wish to express my gratitude to Rachel Breau, M.L.I.S., and to Marissa Barnes, M.A., for their invaluable assistance with the preparation of the manuscript.

ODE ON EMERGING FROM AN OVERDOSE

I

At first there was nothing but nothing, and nothing was dark.

Only the faint whistle of owl or of train, string-silking
Nerve-ticks, otherwise nothing but nothing and darkness.

All is horrible dark, the inside and the out,
Yet does not hurt, but is rather warm and feels
Like a baby does six months before his birth.

All is horrible dark, the inside and the out,
But wait for what might happen: a single bloodburst,
Like a growing bud? A single vein-slice, like
A filament? A single heart-crow, like a new bird?

Is that what is happening? Is there a beat still there
Which, like a sombre gong, can catenate and chain
All other breathing heart-sounds to its chords, and
Change new vibrancies to other kinds of vibrancies
Like nerve and muscle, hip and sinew, thigh?

Is that then happening now? A long slow beat
Called living life, is it peaking now, beginning to crawl,
Beginning to open up the curtains of smooth thought,
Inaugurate the beginnings of intentions, start similes,
Initiate new actions from the mind and temper fused,
Form into violent fragrances new intakes from the air?

And is this what urged my pen into keep moving
In slow and awakening growth now from *Liebestod*, love-death,
The thing people thought was impossible, just in an opera?
And is this what is keeping open and burgeoned,
Stilted sometimes, but mainly florid and lucid and flowered,
The various shoots, orifices, and growths of the tree
Of my growing mind, now that the life is beginning again?

And if so, what comes first, movement or sensation? Sensation:
The opening eye sees, golden in the fledgling light of its opening,
The lights of the hospital ceiling, the dark bars of the walls
Of the high surrounded beds, the hushed movement of orderlies;
It is dead quiet; the silence of the auditory world
Exaggerates the colours of the visual, making yellow gold, blue black,
And green to ultramarine; until a question comes, "Hello,
Do you know where you are?" and I give the answer:

"Yes, I'm in a hospital." And, having given the answer,
I have responded, made movements, become part again of the world,
For in it now I once again move, and each movement,
Speech, thought, or action, becomes the next perceptual trigger
For the next new movement, speech, or thought or action;
And to the visual and auditory worlds enfolds that strange
And half-unrecognizable environment, the kinesthetic,
The feeling of myself *in* motion, feeling my throat,
My sides, my legs, all with their simple and tuned accomplishments.

And then slowly the sensations with the movements start to fuse
Forming what's called the "self"; and the self looks rather than sees,
Acts rather than moves, does rather than thinks, and drops
Corners onto rounded spaces, artefacts onto emptinesses, often
Stupidities onto otherwise beauties; but it is self; and now self
Sees, with the growing stupefaction of sanity (for that means "self"),
That one's self, one's body, that *other* part of one is held
Alive and aloft on a long silver tubing running into an arm;
There are no feelings of inflow or outflow, or of pain;
Just knowledge that one lives intravenously, and here is proof.

And so one tries to be one's self again; one tries to sleep,
But now some new sensations come, of pain; where, in
The early phase of overdose, I had lain with crossed legs
Unthinkingly, there had developed sores; and where, to prevent
Other infections, the doctors had injected, were developed aches
(I refer, of course, in a Rabelais vein, to my rump);
And where, because of the ways that pills and alcohol work

I had become dehydrated, was thirst; and these three
Kept up, in a small chanting chorus of irritation,
Three nasty muses, one might say, fooling with lyres,
Enough incantations to keep me from sleeping and thus lie awake.

And, gradually, stealthy visitors of the night came by:
One to read my temperature, heart-rate, and blood-pressure;
Another to take a new blood-sample, pricking my arm;
Another to say "I am Dr. ..." and that he would see me later;
Another a next-door neighbour wheeled from the operating theatre
Out to recover by my side (I noticed a black eye);
Further over, a baby; and a matron of firm Scottish type
Presiding over bottles and supplies; and somebody (oh dear!)
To change my catheter when it came off when I went,
Which embarrassed me because of the bother but she
Wonderful woman! thought it was funny too; those
Were the first passings of humans athwart my antagonized vision.

And slowly where I had noticed numbness before or nothing,
There came back sentiments of my old self, notably
The unquestioning ease with which I had normally done an action
Like sitting upright or rolling over, how these actions
All depended on interlocking and gearing of neuron and muscle,
Uncontaminated by extra sensations like pain; so that now,
When I could not find a position to easily sleep in,
And rolling over was a slow one-two foxtrot of adolescence
Of movement, watching each muscle emptily work on its own,
I realized far more how important the naturalness
Of our other coordinations are for those more individual
Coordinations of thought that we have to acquire;
And my mind started thinking of movements as signals in noise.

And then there also came back to me lonely emotions,
But all of them seemed in a sense subservient against
One new emotion I had not felt before: that of aliveness.
Even though there was pain and boredom, they were not so bad
As to make me wish I were dead again; instead,

I thought of spring and rebirth, new chances to rejuvenate,
New ways to watch the walks of winter fade away,
New islands out to steer for, new eminences to emulate,
New human beings to love or hate or just endure, but all
Caught in a crazy coruscation, seashell drawn,
In the blue horizon that lay where the slowly dawning day
Cast her white shadows over the last of night's dark clouds;
And this was the emotion that made me forget the cause of my pain,
And this is an emotion that too few people have felt.

And gradually there grew in me over the next few hours
New fire-flintings of the dawn, desires, appetites;
I had not eaten for at least two days, and starved;
And when the breakfast arrived, I ate it as if it were religion;
And when the lunch came later, I studied it like a Druid;
And only the sexual appetite remained unquenched, for I
Did not wish to put more strain on a dark-exerted body;
And the doctors told me more fine details; the nurses
Began to smile again and I to communicate with them;
Visitors came to see me and explain things; and there
Was the presence of flowers, one red, one yellow,
Which stand, as I write, like gorgeous clusters of emeralds
Crowned with rubies and glaring suns; and outside I can see
The still-a-little-cold but smiling lake, laughing
At the way the sky was blue again and living;

And Life itself is hovering above each fern, each tree,
Dotting in fretted halos round each furled leafbud
The fervent ardours and bushelled loads that will be flowers;
And Life is walking about the pavement in the guise of a pigeon
Or a squirrel, ready to imbue with impartial particulars
The needs of each to each animal, ready to meet and embrace,
Ready to grave the earth with yet more of their kind;
And Life walks through waters also, where the fish now begin
To fill the hollows of their underworld, to turn the weeds,
To nuzzle dark poking sticks to minor nests in their brown;
And in the earth, where the insects waken with startled antennae;

And on the earth, where living children walk and stretch the streets;
And over the earth, where birds fling high their hawsered pinions
And sail on wings spun from springsap, joyously singing;
Everywhere Life herself is hovering above each fern, each tree,
And I can stretch myself and yawn and begin to feel born free.

II

For spring obliterates the dark incompetence of winter
And pulls, with fawning light, the darker mantle, darkened green
Over the yellow paltriness of March; the vain thrushes, proud
Of their just rebirth, proud of the nests, the eggs, sit
Upon sharpened branches, scalloped from breath and breathing
Of highest trees, singing in full and glazing canticles;
The swallow zips, swoops, glides, and drops in enticing geometry
Over the selfsame branches that bud and peer into the light
The filtered sun throws through the gloaming clouds;
The first flash of the blackbird's red American wing
Flatters the green of the tiny leaves, and brings in contrast
The florid awakening of rowed tulips to stronger bloom;
The embittered sun, pushing through the clouds, sends angry light
Down in cascades of iron through the overribbed clouds
Like heartbeats, drumbeats of luminance, arrogances of radiance,
Arcades of albedo; and the swift wind, born of the melting summer
Of further south, clasps all these into his halting hands and waits.

And, slowly, the fainting season slowly starts, the incompetence banished,
The fire and the flurry of blood in the veins unsatiated,
With arching limbs and irradiated visions; the night draws back,
Her limpid mists all distant from the fields where light
Now grips and grows across the enchanted horizon; the first
Faint fullcalls of falcons and starlings, robins and redstarts
Fill the faint flush of the fields; the sun stretches and yawns
Through soft and yellow teeth over the distance, smiling at power;
The rankled cloud of night empties away, withdrawn like liquid;
The darkness of insomnia is gone, and fully flooded
Morning makes her smiling bow; the first few flowers

Fold and unfold their radiant petals in the long lush grass;
And the first lamb of Spring, shaking his petulant head,
Empties his first few skipbeats into the air; like other lambs,
The clouds, blown by the May winds, fold, fall, and re-falter
In quietly growing casks, buttresses of storms, battalions of encounter
Over the broad and new blood-breeding blue of the sky
That arcs in broad swordsong over the whole wide land.

Thus, Tartar-like, the growth of new emotion and will and desire,
The *Wiederaufbau* of the soul, from death's slow opening doorway;
The first renewals fresh of sexual power, the first faint conquerings,
The first imagined footfalls of reality, overtures of newness,
Sprawl in their quick cascades through seasoned time, which passes
In new mirror-forms, crisscrossing the dull minutes, making of hours
Full dreams; of seconds, movements; and days to mimicked nights;
Overtoned by plans, each action takes to itself vast borders
Coloured with light and twitching with sensations; each several
Act, trite to the viewer, takes on symbol, just as lechery
Swoons at, yet forswears, the crowd of a congregation; and velvet
Over the way my mind can scoop, into a throw, a day's events, with
The intangibility of history, quiet and profound, moulding the means,
The morals, and the motives of each plan. Across each day
Now lies a moulded tent, a canopy, soft, yet hard as wood,
Which whispers in a quiet re-echoed way that through
A miniature Inferno I have walked without a Virgil guide;
And into the black recesses of my soul I have poured
Flowers, each blushing with the pain of its new colour.

And sometimes Tyrant Sleep calls me away to exotic places
Where flowers grow wild and strange and are accompanied by alligators
Around and through which I swim over seas of confused and coloured
Weeds that blow wild and soft in the sighing sea-surge; rocks
Are uncoloured, being absent, and seem soft; instead, only the
Watchwords of life, flowers and animals, appear to confuse
My sole and dark-degraded image of intention, burdening
Hopes with failing desire or plans with mockeries of imports.
What kind of motley game does Sleep play? With its comedy

Of broken parts, bright brilliant Harlequins, and always absent
Columbines, what kind of game is it that Slumber strikes me
Softly about the head with, like a potter's hammer, or the glaze
That sometimes cracks, or flows, or glosses, and sometimes
Melts into solid form, unglinting when the sun shines? It is
The game of the Intention versus the Need; the horror of Ego
Against the Desire, the mockery of the Plan against the Reality;
And it glides its awninged path through these; the Life-Force
Speaks and acknowledges incompetence, acknowledges littleness;
And the wild Ego shrieks, and it breaks its head against mirrors
And starts abashed thereafter, till Sleep completes the picture.

Or then again momentary Delight, be it the unexpected touch
Of me against the flower-gown of a sixteen-year-old girl
Born with dark eyes that flatter me in Age; or the soft
Touch of a madwoman, knowing her power, and dreaming of
A sweet fulfillment but tormented by guilt; or the look of
An old and stained fifty still conscious of desire; or the
Lesser momentum of other senses, taste and smell and sight;
All of these are watchwords pulling me on to where I think
Maybe Goethe went, to where the Eternal-Womanly pulled
Him along, *das Ewig-Weibliche zieht uns hinan*; and
Delight fused with Sleep causes empty morning torment,
A blues of unfulfillment, confusion of the temporary;
And, like a vivid image, I can stand and fall back as if
I had conjured the Spirits of the Dead or of the Stars,
As Manfred conjured evil from his Alps; and I on a lonely
Self-girt mountain stand and gaze on imagined stars,
Hoping to pull and conjure from one's fire the blue
And opal denizens of the planets, the red and emerald
Scarlets of the Universe, hoping to draw, in one swift blade,
Sweet conjured fire, the living fire I saw when, wide awake,
I saw my own Astarte fused with Proserpine and life.

Or Mentation, who wanders with fore-and-aft cloaked deliberation
Stretching across even life-objects' beauty, like the patterns of a flower,
The interlocking spirals of the seeds on its head, or the rhythm

Of petals; or the quick walk of the horse, or the trot captured
Photographically in several segments of magnanimous movement;
Or the delicacy of a Hydra's tentacle swimming with venom,
Laid out and launched in accordance with neurological law;
Or the perfection of a great History, with the events akimbo
And kings watching laughter descend down centuries; all of these
Come into the basket of Mentation, provider of peace,
Example, elegance, and immutability. Is thought not Thought?
Is to be conquered by a theorem's beauty no achievement?
Is to be vanquished into silence by the perfection of
A ctenophore or rhadamanthine ocellus, no joy?
Is there not conquest in the analysis of a ray, a bubble,
A light-spark, a foam? Is there not victory in the unraveling
Of a formula, a molecule, or the successful descent into the Atom?
All of these fall into the full and factful arms of *Veritas*,
Sweet-blind model for youth, the wide and nailed truncheon
Of Intention, the Obliterator and Destroyer of self, the weighted
Nemesis of theory, the parched antagonist of the irreversible,
The ployed and plotted avalanche of the egotistic unbeauty.

Or Art, in whose enticing arms the solstices of emotions meet,
And bracket into crystal offerings wild barns of grain and gold,
Summit and nadir, apostrophe and incumbency, sungold and darkness,
All to a solid jewel of wonderlessness? Can I find life in Art?
Can I find life where man has taken sounds, chopped from them tunes,
Filled palaces with melancholy lutes or halls with blazing horns?
Can I find life where statues stand sculpted from marble, the knees
Of achievement, breasts of competence, visages all filled with fire
Or tortured into Laocoön? Can I find life where paint has been
Poured into silver vials, and sketched and orbed, been flourished
Trumpet-like into a square, been ladled into sylvan nymphs
Or monotonic portraits? Can I find life where ruby jewels
Have been finely niched into silver and gold, to tiny coaches?
Can I find life where moulded parts, rising in absorbance from
The moving potter's fingers, slowly take their final form
And achieve with the turn of the ring-finger, the vetted
Light of a vase or the overwhelming curvature of a bowl

Potted in bull-shape? Can I find life where words on words
Are scored into monstrous paragraphs, narrations of bolder loves
Then mine, more fretted by experience, more tinged with mockery
Or morals, more real by being unreal? Or can I even
Find life where words are forced and folded, folded into
Long quiet scans of verses such as these, or quieter?

Or let, instead of mental creations, something more like fire come,
Source unsought-for, unquenched flickering and flaming; let us imagine
A tree whose flaring branches are flames, whose roots are flickered
Fire-tongues, whose leaves small white sparks or flares; let us
Conceive that this tree exists, on a rock, the sea below it;
The sea turns, enchanted against the raw red beauty
Of the tree its wave-eyes see, and throws and hurls
Its rippled arms into the rock's enclosures; the sky hangs,
Low and lowering with thunder, against the great red flare;
And the green sea beneath, black and grey and streaked
In white, hurls its enchanted orations against the unquivering rock.
What kind of tree would so stand, eager and powerful, haunted,
Against the sea-sky background unpainted? Is *it* Art?
Is *it* Mentation? Is *it* Delight? Is *it* Sleep? It is more,
Not one of these; rather they grow from it; their source is it;
Their enlightenment is it; it inspires *them*; it moves *them*;
It is *their* light; it is *their* fruit. See how it grows, grows
As the sea hurls against it like a gull brought and
Down-hovered from the distant abyss of that ocean; see how,
As the gull nears it, shrieking, it sends out one longer arm,
One more powerful flame; and the gull hurtles itself against it,
Is nearly burned, nearly scorched, and nearly falls to the sea;
But is instead fed, and is brought to new fullness, and retracts;
The heaven-gull is fed from Hell, and fire is its true nourishment.

For that tree is the source-fruit, the *Ur*-original seed, the flame
That forms all other sides and aspects of life; it is both frame
And inner picture, both luminance and light, both tone and generator;
From this original source, energy flames; from this comes power;
And just as light is the epitome and final outcome, the emergent

Of fire and flame—just as sound results from vibration—as touch
Results from contact—so that fire-flame, whose name is Passion,
Energizes all sources of mind, life, love, literature, and novelty.
And thus we all pass from infancy to Age; at first, the quiet
Emptiness of growth, the halting walk, the accented tongue,
The shimmered words whose grammar-form is love, the looks,
The quiet unburgeoned contact of infants, boy, girl; then,
The growth, the socialization, the origins of groups, and the mental
Mind deliberating, pondering on the origins of evil in the crowd;
Then the sudden spurt of seed, adolescence, the trembling, the
Catching on silver platters of memorabilia like birthdays, the
Organization of improvements of contact, the terrible shudder,
The holy choir disorganized by sex, the appalling enticements,
With parents like older grinning dogs ready to snap; and the
Fuller enticements of greater maturity, with love put first,
And all else second, even if unrequited; then, for some,
But not for most, the completion of Twoness and the complete
Control of the fire, taken and burned into either's body;
And finally the desecration of old Age, the observation of
The beauty insurgent of young bodies, wasted for not enough love.

Love is held back, for some, for too long. Every incitement
Is there in Society, yet Death sits on the young and watches greed
Turn into nothing, society turn into nothing, achievement turn,
Yes, into nothing; and only Passion giving life. The old know this;
The old see clear; their bodies are purged; and the young ones wait
Also for the purgation, the purification, of thorough and sexual being.
And so Death, like Passion, sits and waits for the destruction thereof.
He is tall and dark, and capable of smiling; he holds within
His gold and sceptered hand the relative roles of incumbent,
Author, bishop, or priest; his hands control life; and life snarls
At him like a tiger. Passion snarls at Death. Love spits on Death.
Life hates Death. Death is a grinning idiot, a small darkness,
And life, which is Passion, is a live tree of fire. Life
Can laugh if in Passion. Life without Passion is Death. Life
Without Passion is Mortification. Mortification is Death. Frustration
Is Death. Life with Frustration is Death. Life is Love, and Love, Life.

Love without Frustration is Life. Love with Passion is Life.
Life with Passion is Love. Love with Life hates Death.
Love without Death is Life. Love with Frustration is Death.
Death stands and breathes on his hollow fingers. He is mortified.
Death has been laughed at. Death has been laughed at by Love.
Death has been mocked by Love. Death has been approached
By Frustration. Love is Life and Life is Love. Life lives,
Love loves, Death dies. Love has laughed at Death. Love
Is alive, and forswears Death. Death is only a place.
It is a place where nothing is Nothing and Nothing is dark.

PURSUIT

August

Morningscape: 5 a.m.

It's 5 a.m. and Venus is still there,
A steadfast tininess within her night;
The first non-crushing sounds of trucks and cars
Pass upwards to where my window's open a chink,
And the silent streetlights marching up the hill
Waver impassively while branches move
Their lights as if they waved to me.
This is so quiet and still a night today:
We have had storms and wind, clouds, rains, and insects,
But today is all calm, a day when calm and moonlight
Are totally in absentia because
Daytime is due, when the prized sunrise's arms
Of pink battalions and of shaded gold
Have spread their probing fingers up the hillside
Hopefully, a foretaste of fruition.

Morningscape: The Moon Is Real

There *is* a moon; I'd thought it a reflection,
In the window-glass, of one of my ceiling-lights,
But, no, I blotted out the latter with my hand,
And still the moon shone, stuck in place, and firm
As a corolla frozen round a rim of sunfire.
The moon is the symbol of my mind's Selena,
Something bright, but brightening less than Sun,
Something firm, but yielding, faintly palpable,
To the licks and touches of the staring stars;
The moon is sign, it has been said, of madness,
Yet by others is made songstress of the noon,
Accompanist to lyrics sung by June,
A liquid laugh of the glorious word called "soon";
And, even as I look again, from writing this,
A faintish halo signals that morning's nearer
And soon will obliterate the moon's appearance.

Morningscape: August

A coffee I crave as now my words die out
As an August morning, crystal-grey and clear,
Slowly makes shine the outline of the hill
Over which creep the streetlights, shining still
And silent upon as yet untraveled roads;
But rooftops now seem grey and sharp in the light,
And, in the distance, boldly the lake
Stretches, like an inland Adriatic,
Off to the West like a striding roustabout.
No sunlight as yet is *dancing* off its waves;
But its glint speaks of soonness and of savoury
Momentousnesses I have never known,
And my dawn-sunglint seems to be my own
As if I fled from Nature to pursue it.

Morningscape: Vista

There's one red tree that stands alert out there,
But, as I sat to write those syllables down,
A window pane's location in my view
Changed, and I saw a brighter red I thought
Must be a sign or roof or tent, until
I looked and saw it was a redder tree,
But, by contrast, redder it seemed, because
Its red was partial, a bright near-floral growth
On just a small subtended clustering
Of branches on one side of a tree, the side
That looked south-east to where, so far away,
Were the stands and stalls and shining cylinders
Of a glistening New York. Now, tell me pray,
Where are the people in my poem for today?

Morningscape: Wakening

How can a swathe of yellow in this autumn light
Catch my eye as a female would who was on the go?
Green retains its power as the colour of the hill;
But slowly the reds are beginning to creep and climb and grow;

The sky still has a blue as if summer still were here;
As the sun rises, darkening clouds slip slowly down
Until the sun has reached highness and, unclouded, shines
Over a countryside filled with the noises of town;

Slowly the town awakes, with sounds of cars and planes;
A train emits, harmlessly clanking, a chuff
Before it pulls, languorous and efficient, into
A station where people, hardly awakened enough,

Wait to sit down on the train to look, through its windows, outside
At the reds, and occasional yellow, that tell them that summer has died.

September

Glow

The first dark tinge of red has set its glow
On the darker and deeper greens of the sloping hill;
Harbinger it is of frosty nights
Where the reds will glow and flame into fires until
Their errantry is stopped by the fall of the snow;

A fire, however, upon a smoky hill
Is symbol, not only of Fall, but of broadening views
That lurch like vistas or landscapes or sights
Caught and embellished by fires that the light imbues
With reds resplendent and lit with light, until

The reds have exploded and vanished underneath
The winter that pierced the roots and trees of the wood;
Scandalizing the verdancies of the heath
Are words of wanting for Thee and for Thy Good.

Too Near

I cannot speak,
For far too near to me
Appears thy lovely cheek;

I have no voice,
For thy appearance
Steals from me any choice;

I have no rhymes
To flatter thee with, so
Fraught am I at those times

When you're so near
That the world all telescopes
To mistiness clear.

Quiet Comes the Sun

Quiet comes the sun; a barricade
Of blue curtain acts as a blind
That breaks its inflicting brightening
And lets a softer glow inside;

The sun is like you, you are melody made,
And the warmth that you spread has a tempered kind
Of brightness, a sprightly lightning,
To revive what was in me that had died.

Artspeak

I cannot sleep for fervent thoughts of thee.
The brown of your soft near-suit will always be
The first of my thoughts, forever, of your form.
Slenderness gives your figure a splendour thine,
A boy-like eloquence in a Columbine.

How can I *not* write things like this to thee?
When first I saw you, distanced, away from me,
I thought *I* had designed your perfect form.
Over the distance stretched a floor you stalked.
Its carpet trembled gently as you walked.

Its corridor walls were *Vogue*-like packaging.
Its atmosphere accomplished a ravaging
Of my mind as you walked, a model of purist form,
A paradigm of what I'd dared not seek.
I'd never dreamed of a loveliness so unique.

My Apartment

I heard, through walls not over-thick, the sound
Of the elevator door; 'twas 6:00 a.m.,
And the sound signaled the newspaper's arrival,
Bringing new knowledge we needed for survival
In the cut-and-thrust kill-world of our adult classes
Now that the papers, at last, had suddenly found
That research on the mind intrigued the reading masses
More than research on matter had interested them.

My love for you possesses a ferocity
No newsprint-acres ever have reported.
Their pages are filled with life and with iniquity,
But I see their lines as blurry and distorted,
Because, hovering over them, thy Thee
Has fused with Life, but not yet fused with me.

Transcendence

The nights have worked their magic, and my mind
Is clear like the clarities of clear blue skies
That flicker across September's end and find
Flowers with new colours, sparkling their surprise,

Goldens and purples, wildflowers many, a mix
With a radiance of mingling and song
That spikes with refreshment this Autumn. To fix
The best of the summer's endings and prolong

Those summer's endings deep into winter's bay,
A ship of transcendences shall slide on streams
Between remorses that had never blown away,
And pushed by headwinds based on lifelong dreams;

Your beauty breathes so loudly in my ear,
It devastates the bell that says you're here.

Corridors

No better cause have I than wanting Thee;
Through corridors that run between apartments,
Thou walkest with ineffable perfection,
And I must search Thy proud implacable face
For signs of increments in Thy affection;
Round me the walled corridors keep their place,
Flat in agreement that nothing's holding me
From fumbling with the wealth of your *accoutrements*

Except the fear I lose all that I hope from Thee;
So I look, glumly, at carpets and at coverings
That hide the solid floor from Thy moving feet,
Walling it off from secrets indiscrete
That could emerge from its discoverings,
Were it to *feel* your feet, of ecstasy.

You, Seated

How vulnerable, lovely, tough, and human
You are, seated just where you think that I
Can't see you (and, in truth, do not); my seeing
Is meagre in perception of the now;
It's counterpart to a pitch black night that Hope
Stops and starts and hurls and pitches out
Into oblivious *rendezvous*
Where you, renegade within the power
Of your appeal within that darkness, sit,
While I, staring at you, not yet inviting
You, see you transmuted to a Night
In which these mental winds of mine inflate
The fading dark of you to blazing light,
And the growing black of you to winsomeness.

Venture

What cannot be caught
In verse or in rhyme
Is how tactless touch
Can teach so much
That cannot be taught;

A wisp of your hair,
Soft and sublime
Touched my palm
As it dropped to the calm
Of your hip-line where

Haunch met at waist;
I felt a climb
Of something unsought
That can never be taught
Or disgraced.

Longing

I am longing to go now and fall into your arms,
But the guarded ambience about your head
Tells me that those vestiges of a dread
That spur you cold, quite rob *me* of my charms;

I image thee, becrested with a spark
Of electric hair above your lovely head,
An image of half-crazed lamentation-dread
That springs from me as I lie in a lonely dark;

And, in that dark, I do not dare to steal
A glance at the guessed-at opulence of thy head;
I fear what whirlpools might enhance my dread
Of non-enchantment that you can't conceal;

So I flinch, and hide my wide and wondering eye
'Neath the bedclothes dark while the moon goes pottering by.

Colours

There is a rift near-tropical
Between the colours of sky and lake;
Dark it had been, and blustery,
But a blast of sun had blazed to make

A drizzly grey to a bronzing green
On the sea-wide surface of the lake,
Symbol that storms can leave both clouds
And dazzling colours in their wake.

Closeness

As the rain falls and greyness seems to cloud
The air that's circulating close to me
And to a misted landscape that I see
Enveloped in the rainfall like a shroud,

I see that greyness as a masterpiece
Designed to prove that every day that's dull
Is really waiting, close, to re-enthrall
My self with a newfound sense of new release.

Cross Grain

To know, with a suddenness, that she might be "yours"
Gives counter-grain to what I wrote elsewhere;
I wrote* I had no right to call her "mine,"
But now I feel, with a sudden surge of calm,
That calling you "mine" allows you to call me "yours";

And so, in this cross-grained frame, I look and see
You as a will, reflecting, mirror-like,
My will, with hidden sounds moving and surging
To smite the sunderedness and thus to make
You into a me, both mirrored as an "us";

And I feel fear *because* I feel no fear;
Fear, I wrote**, was a tell-tale of romance;
So, what *are* these enchanted surenesses
That you are there, and stay there while I look
At you, and you look at me back? Realities?

---

*   *Celebrations and Other Poems*, p. 116
** *Surface Tension and Other Poems*, p. 58

Requiredness

Words are so few that supply the many meanings
I want to convey when my mind is full of you
That, in my tactile visioning of your sloping shoulder
And adorable fall of your hair on to its sloping breadth,
Only anatomy jumps into my stammering consciousness;
What else I think is a gap requiring a requisition,
A vagueness desperate for wealth, for fitness, and for
A detailed disquisition on what I dare not dream;
I can imbue all my mind's presently present contents
With colours or phrases or tangled mingled concerns,
But none of them give what I want in this aching diffusion,
This raddled inequity, this stifled and searching confusion;
Rampant and redolent within this evasive effusion
Is a jerky and halting lament for an unfused infusion.

October

Hopes

The reds are beginning and the sea
Has a frozen look (a trick of the sky)
(I meant the lake, not the sea)
... This is a prose I cannot reason by!

The reds restart and the silver lake
Burns with a pregnancy likely to be
The start of a winter where I make
Widening words into poesy;

I hope my words can fuse, and do not gash
My skies with unprecedented fears;
May turbulences start to slash
All cowardice from my wordy tears!

I hope that words that please will come my way;
I hope I can please *you* every single day.

Strand in Distance

A sense of the truth and rightness of your being
Came after rain, when the sky grew light again,
And a low and sunlit barrier of cloud
Revealed a lake of greys and blues and silvers
That stopped at its far-off edge in a single line,
A grey that marked the meeting of lake with strand,
Rarely seen, but now clear-cut, though faint,
A resting place for tired and weary hopes
That the righteous deadliness of singlehood
Would find conciliation in that land,
A far and distant, yet existent, place;
And this far distant, greyish line of land
Promises remissions from life's brutishness,
And a sombre sense of landfall in *my* life.

A Trick of the Light

In any kind of surge of sonic splendour,
There always appears to me your female hair,
Fresh but wispy in curious side-lit curls
That only a trick of lighting shows are there;

And, in an elevator, your back against a mirror,
I see your splendid form and want to move
To hold you, but do not; I fear my ardour
May hurt what you may feel for me of love.

For Every Moment

For every moment that you even breathe
I feel transgression of my inward vow;
A sigh in your voice suffices to bequeath
To that moment an everlasting Now;

A little joy that puckers up your eye,
A tiny glisten of a mortal tear,
Turn my endeavouring verses rocket-high,
Pull my bewildered fantasies too near;

A glance up at your softened misted glance
And I cannot breathe because I love you so;
And a turn of timely phrase can re-advance
The moves that I had stopped for fear you'd go;

Oh, how can Fate have done this awful thing,
To bring me a want for you that is so strong
That everything inside me wants to sing
An endless never-ending endless song?

Wind-Stop

Windless the world seems when the waves are quiet;
Blueness is endemic to the lake; and brightly green
Are the trees flaunting their lightness against
The darker greens against the reds of roofs.
But how they are rare, my almanacks of you
Leaning, for just a moment, against me,
Or tapping, just for a moment, my sleeved arm,
Gently to shake its solicitude away!
Oh, how I want to solder more than was,
To put together more than was there before,
To anchor, in a sort of soft soliloquy,
Something of you to something of me, as if
The heavens were to bend, spontaneous,
And bless, with affection, any tactile move.

Wind-Moment

You were so lovely, I thought I could be bold
And let the wind that surged and flapped your hair
Manoeuvre itself around mine; but I failed to wear
The hat that would keep me distanced from the cold;

Entranced with you was I, and could not move
My eyes from you to scan the sundry skies
That breathed their elements upon your eyes,
Flecking them with tints as if to prove

That you were one with all the elements;
I was brought back some fifty years to when
I was walking in a moor-like Scottish glen
And saw the sky break into rudiments

Of ruddy colours under a veil of black;
But here, I feel the cold I'd caught come back.

Wind-Breath

When the lake is mild and the wind is calm,
Black signals betray the presences of waves;
They cluster the vista from near to furthest far,
Symbols of how a wind-breath the water moves;

And *that* is symbol of how *your* finest breath
Flutters the muttering vestiges of my mind
Into o'erflattering versicles to Thee
That scarcely footings in the Real can find.

Wind-Howl

Oh, how the wind howls! Howls wind a clock
Whose minutes scratch their scrawniness on Time,
While nothing but seconds tick on and on and on
And silent howls wind up their carillon.

O Time, how wanton thou art, with all thy tongues
Martyring moments of hope with promises,
While heartbeats mutter and murmur, diapason
Against the shame of being a minion

Of usury where Time is a borrowed thing,
Taken from lifetime's own trajectory,
Where Quiet is vista of oblivion,
And Sleep to Rest bears no comparison;

A baring of Time shows us no skeleton,
No warmth, no throat, no thing to lean upon.

Dress Code

Brilliant, like coloured candies, stand the trees;
Each, in its isolate yellow or orange or red,
Stands, incarnate like a flame, astride
Velveted verdures of summery greens that squeeze,

From the reds, sundered scarlets, from oranges, flares,
And, from yellows, exquisite banners that blow
Robustly amidst the breezes; the colours flow
Like a seasonal dress that the onset of winter wears.

Notspeak

Although I thought I'd maybe die
Here in this bower of hills and lake,
My meeting you has forced my hand
Longevity measures now to take;

I'll walk some more and fantasize
All the more when you're not here;
I'll eat more greens and less dessert,
And turn my thinking into clear

And clarified logics for to be
Nearer to you in inner thought;
But, were I to say all that out loud,
All that I said might count for naught.

Thinking of You

Although the night is growing late,
I do not want to go to bed;
I'm tired of lying there thinking of you;
I want to be holding you there instead;

How empty it is, my lonely room.
Others may come and make it more
Like the room of a girl I used to know
Who had had many men in the past, before

I had crested the billowing waves of her bed,
Filling with warmth each corner of her,
And the room, and her bed, and of me, in a bold
And monomaniac fury and stir;

But my feelings for you quite override
Any fancies of somebody else at my side.

November

Leaves

Now are the grounds all filled with falling leaves
And Cupid, like a laser, shoots up high
At a blue that covers, in sheets of blue,
All of the verity that is the sky;

Mind locked with matter fuses, falls, and spells
Litanies of lines that laud the sky;
Now lie the leaves pathetic on the grounds,
But soon will stand proud, but nobody knows why.

Heart-Clutch

Wrote Joseph Conrad in *Lord Jim*,
"A teaspoon fell like a tiny scream";
A tiny scream I won from you
When I told you where I'd seen you wear
The skirt you wore with me today;
You screamed because you'd learned my care
For you went to where I'd seen you wear
That skirt; 'twas rather far away;
In a crowd it was that I first saw you
Walking in speed-walk, skirt aflare,
Straight through a throng so serious-minded
That I was the only one you blinded
And dazzled as you walked straight through
A crowd so thick with unimportance
That you and your skirt were agencies
Of boldness and oh! such braveness.

How Do I Feel?

A brilliant yellow stripes the high horizon,
A hint that winter's cloudland's looming near;
Below the gold the lake reflects the greyness
Of the mighty cloudbank as it moves up here;

I dare not write that you may mellow, like
The glorious infiltrate of cloud by sun;
I dare not write that you are softening to me
When so much, so much there is that must be done;

I dare not write the overlift of greyness
That keeps you fettered to your desk or chair
May lift, and you stand up, and move towards
My hesitating self; I'm too aware

That a minor move of charitable touch
On my part could reharden you twice as much.

Diamond

This is a night like a diamond solitaire,
So solidly does it shine, as if conviction
Burnished its lustre and caused its cuts to glow
And its facets to wink with coloured articles
As the light of the night shines upon its stone,
Lighting the night's luminance
Black, as if black were white and crystalline;

This is a night of *sitting*, writing, thought;
Where is the bed, the vaporous bath, the steam,
The firmament of reality and not of dream,
The anxious-makingness of first-night fears,
The traipsing of the drama o'er the scene?
Incongruous are these thoughts; improbable is
An outcome stretching far into eternity.

Surprises

When precious things are not discussed
For fear their loss will taint the whole,
Then does a door open quietly out
To let one in, into one's own soul;

And, in one's soul, surprises spring;
One finds in there an Endymion,
A beauteous body flaunting want,
And hungry to be fed upon;

And she who mildly knocks to ask
If come in she can is shocked to see
How all her smallnesses seem giant
Enticements to his lechery

The whiles his greying hair betrays
A waning of want in his waning days.

Hiatus

I have two nights in which Thou art not here,
So cloud them over with phantasmic thought,
Stare at the chair where you may never be
On overnight, gaze at a blinking aeroplane
In the air, see how the table sits without
A partner, watch how the dishes overpile,
Before being filed away in emptiness,
And stare at nothing save your gazing ghost.

But what electric flarings sheet from it!
Thine is the balustrade to awkward power,
A target like an infinite climbing-tower,
Portrayal of the animal in me
(But not the beast), scanner of charms, and planner
Of monuments and ceremonials
Written upon with scourges made of ink
And delicate touches chiseled in like linen.

Softness

Of a perfection of flesh, I scarcely dare speak;
Yet it is incumbent on me, poet as well as lover,
To write how my first full handful of your head,
Its hair falling to each side, like arbitrate from God,
Was softer, less hard of bone, unexpected
Had I ever dared to expect anything otherwise,
And a soft pullulation of perfection marred
My hand, so soft and lovely felt your head;
Even the gentlest of gentlest content, a kiss
Of gratitude so short it made my gratitude greater,
Fell on a softness firm and delicate like the arms
Of goddesses holding up arms of admiration
Upon Olympus, up in Helicon, for heroes,
Holding them high, their softness substituting
For compassion and their loveliness for empathy.

I Have No Appetite

I have no appetite for less than Thee,
For less than your sparkling eyes and lively face,
Shoulders soft-spotted with imperfect skin,
Arms with an elbow somewhat scratched,
Fingers that know how to hold a brush
To scrub the sediment from a coffee cup,
And hips all hidden 'neath your outer clothes,
And legs I do not dare to dream upon,
Or touch in unawakened semi-sleep,
And toes that run tidily over the floor,
Unheeding what scattered toys lie underfoot,
And toenails quite untouched with lacquer,
And a nothing then arrived at save a sigh
That I forgot your brain when I began.

December

Holiday

If absence makes the heart, as claimed, grow fonder,
Why is your absence so disheartening?
The dream I had of bearing you up yonder
Into a wonder-world is flattening

Into something far less mystical, far more
Of a common sense and clinical, practical kind;
How could you ever be somebody I could ignore?
How ever do so unless I were clinically blind?

Where are you now, my girl from yesterday?
Where is your smile, the bends and the folds of your limbs,
Your tipsy-top torrent of wonderful words at play,
Your seeming pre-knowledge of all my arrogant whims?

I think that your absence has made my imagination
Rear, into months, the days you were off on vacation.

Nearness

Every minute brings me nearer
To the second when we face again
Each other, each perhaps the dearer
To the other, more devoid of pain;

Every hour that brings us nearer
Seems like a rivet bolted into Time;
What is thought now will never be clearer,
Nor ever more likely to burst into rhyme;

Every noon that brings us nearer
Seems to epitomize Time as dead;
Time *was* Distance's standard-bearer,
But now is Proximity's figure-head;

But every minute of every day,
I also fear you'll go away.

January

Panorama

The streetlights look like Christmas lights
Scattered about the town;
The level of lightness goes way up
As the winter sun goes down;

A January panorama
Hides within its cold
Packages beneath a cloud
That tells that what they hold

Are hopes that were hoped when Fall was here,
Hopes that Winter would bring
A surrogate Summer of promises
To usher in the Spring;

Alas, poor poet, it's only you
Who can make a nectar from frozen dew.

Winterscape

Today I looked out, nothing pre-planned,
At my balcony and saw that the lake
Had frozen to ice that sprawled and spanned
Its east to west without a break;

It was not frozen yesterday;
Overnight cold had gripped its soul,
Turning its waves and moonlight-play
Into a single solid whole;

And then my eye moved to the snow
That littered my balcony with white,
And saw two bootprints made by you
That had stood, unsullied, through the night;

And I nearly wept for want of you;
There was the proof that you'd been here,
Two bootprints staring from the snow,
A proof decisive, strong, and clear.

Onslaught

I have braved thee and thy onslaughts on my mind:
The beauty with which your waist twists as you turn,
The somewhat vacant remnants of your bangs
That brought me back into a Paradise,
The eager limpidities of your sweet brown eyes,
Filled with a moving meaning, pulling me
Into your Heaven of a smile, unbarring Hope;

Thee I can write about, feeling, within,
Pullings and tusslings within my wholesome flesh
That I conceal, or, rather, integrate
Into lines like these, so flat upon the page
That their lack of depth exaggerates
The coruscations of my fantasies
On seeing you turn, your waist twisting a-near me.

From Room to Room

Today's another day when heartlessness
Seems to roam, from room to room, till noon,
When my mind begins to fill with artlessness,
Waiting, naively, for the afternoon

When you will walk, in your perceptiveness,
Towards my doorway, blithely stepping in,
And I am torn silly by your receptiveness
To what I teach, but not what I put in.

Zoo in January

In zoos I think I feel at home,
But you feel slightly ill;
The lion surveys his kingdom,
And the leopard, on his hill,

Casts his yellow envious eyes,
With slits to let the light in,
Over a terrain that lies
Flung to the furthest mountain;

But that is the zoo of an *Africaine*,
Not the Zoo *you*'ll visit;
The snow will sallow the ground again,
And winds the trees inhabit;

Cold will the ice be on the pond
Where you the migrant birds may see;
And you may not be as over fond
Of the grizzly as you thought you'd be;

But you would shudder at all that life
Cooped up in all its majesty;
And try to hide your inner strife
Beneath a veil of chivalry.

Portrayals

I saw a monkey on a tree; 'twas just
My altered recollection of a day
When, in Jamaica, I saw an agile black
Who climbed a palm tree in the hopeful trust
That photographers would snap him and would pay
For the kudos of taking their several snapshots back
To prove to their friends at home that they'd been away
To a jungle land where jungle drums held sway.

And, just like those tourists, I also find that I,
Searching, bleakly, for something I can say
To others about my cherishing of you,
Want to hold up a memory to the sky
Of you as a female to whom I dare to pray,
And have each prayer granted as if it had been two,
To prove to my absent friends that I'd been away
To a land where positivity held sway.

But then come realities, earnest, fierce, and fast;
There's nothing, to you, that I have been able to say
That has tempted you to hold me in an embrace
That is more than a hug, and that's also meant to last,
And to burn your mental being to mine in a way
Tendered by you with unornamented grace,
A refined, collected, intelligent display
Of affection for me that had always held *some* sway.

"If" Revisited

If you can grab your woman too abruptly,
If you forget that her birthday is today,
If you assume your desire for her is equaled
By her desire for a romp with you in the hay,
If you dare think a fuzzy morning stubble
Turns her right on, and that she desires you more,
If you assume that it is her bounden duty
To have the dishes done the night before,
If you dare think that your mind analytical
Is prejudice-free and objective more than hers,
And that her place is really in the kitchen
And not among *élites* or *raconteurs*,
Then you will trail behind her in the mall,
While she looks out for someone rich and tall.

February

Another Revisitation

How have I loved thee? Let me list one time:
I loved thee when thy head did droop awhile,
So heavy was the burden of the knowledge-weight
Thrust upon your eager mind by me, who'd been
In your place once, trying to reconcile
My family's needs with students' needs; I'd packed,
Into days, a few weeks' work to demonstrate
That being away from home was not obscene,
Nor undomestic library work a crime;
And my head had drooped, like yours, when, through the ice
Of a freezing rain, I had lugged my books, begirt
By anger because I was putting on an act:
I was pretending, to my students, I felt nice,
And hid, at home, how much my learning hurt.

Your Voice

I listened to your voice with concentration
When you spoke up at a meeting's disputation;
I sought to hear how your consonantal diction
Consolidated was with the conviction
Of your vocalic musics, and how glottal
Stoppings ne'er disturbed the fricatives
That sang sonatas from your sage rebuttal;

You hold a purity of sound within
Your voice, and you guessed that, maybe, it might win,
One day, a medal for its attractiveness to
Someone who felt attractedness to you,
And who guessed, as well, that your bravery lay in your seeing
That maybe, out there, there might, well, never be
A someone who loved your *every* inch of being.

But I am that someone, you brave and lonely girl!
I am that someone who'd positively boil
With ecstasy your lovely voice to hear,
And, in a fusion I admit is none too clear,
To grip it and hold it and kiss it! But discontent,
That I've waited so long to try to enhance
Your beauty of sound, has left me somewhat spent.

More on Your Voice

It's a quarter to one on a Sunday afternoon,
And I should be eating lunch, but find instead
That, running like daydreams through my foggy head,
Is the voice of a friend with whom I'd talked on the phone.

She had phoned me to join her for music once again,
After absence of years; and, because of that,
I'm writing this poem as if, at the drop of a hat,
Words, once again, were flying from my brain;

Horror! Sing they to her voice, not to yours?
O my adored and belaboured newcomer, please
Do not think of this poem as one designed to tease;
It is moulded to fit (and befit) your elegant ears;

Only a brand new Muse, like yours, can make
A poet more respectable, for poetry's sake.

Monolith

Plots and plans and behemoths,
River horses from the Nile,
Come to disturb the eloquence
That freely flowed when, lacking guile,

I modeled thee as a monolith
Sculpted of versifying stone,
With odes for bricks, and named, after you,
"Perfection," a concept all my own

From ideologies made, and hopes,
And memories improperly laid;
And, on its base, I'd carved my lines
To Thee, preferring not to trade

Those lines for words of truth and quiet,
Or stanzas skirting the Ideal;
Although "Perfection" will stay in my head,
Your imperfections are just as real.

February

Oh, my beloved beauty, here I go,
Writing again, while the falling snow
Blankets each branch with a silvery coat of white,
And animals huddle well into night;

February's start is here, and nearer
The Spring will be, when the sky will be clearer;
Its overarching canopy of blue
Will be a coverlet for you.

Greetings

A nonentity target of when you might be here—
"Wednesday perhaps" or "Friday"—is a game
Where every day and yesterday are the same,
Empty and confused with nothing clear;

Thee I have sought down centuries in my mind,
Someone to say hellos to, but not good-byes
Of the interruptive kind that compromise
A Wednesday's or a Friday's being assigned

To your being here for sure; you are a sprite
Who plays with my books, but also spots the ways
I hope to keep you here until such days
As Wednesdays or Fridays fuse, despite

Moments when nonentities like "soons"
Conspire to end those days on afternoons.

Resting Place

Dare I concede you are my resting place,
My haven when society rebels
At the sight of me because my story tells
How a no one can rise to be a someone from disgrace,

From madness and drunkenness fit to fell a mule,
And over-obsessiveness so overdone,
That anyone who finds they're getting on
With me, soon finds they've found a fool?

Only in hiding, close to my wonderful you,
Can I feel safe, untrammeled and unruffled by
The gossip that seems to hang about the sky
Where e'er I walk; but when the sky turns blue,

And freedom distills its ardour from the air,
Letting me flood you with the cataracts
That you release in flood waves, with your acts
Of kindness, and your simple flair

For looking right and talking right, and your speech
Enthusiastic workaholic so like mine,
That I am tempted to bloat you to divine,
But that's a dump land I don't want to reach.

My Calendar

My calendar is covered with your name;
It glows like a lotus in a silver frame
While the dull days are ticketed, one by one,
With things I want to do but haven't done;
But always your name shines through to me,
Like an emerald on a terebinth tree,
Whenever a day stands when you will appear,
Star-like, ambient in the atmosphere,
Until you stand, because it's time to stop,
And I just want to hold you and to drop
To the floor a-with you, but do not,
And off you go after I have got
My nurturing hug, my reminder of when
I'll see your name in my calendar again,
Rising triumphant like a lily from a sea
Jabbed and bewildered with chalcedony,
A lovely bluish-white and precious stone
Fit to adorn you, and only you alone.

Besotted

I am besotted by you as you stand,
Firm in the doorway, while a gentle wind
Gently moves your hair as if to rescind
All inner turbulence; you command,

With your slight and pliant stature, all I need
To flame ecstatic at your wind-moved hair,
And its communication, through the air,
That what I crave, in thought or word or deed,

Is to sing to you high blazon of my want
To hold you and steal you from the wind's display
Of your hair and beauty, steal you quite away
To a place at my side, where I'd be free to flaunt,

As only one who loved you dare deploy,
These cobwebb'd spindles of my wordy joy.

March

White Was the Light

Today sunshine blazed across the lake;
Cold winds had blustered to a final halt;
No longer were walkways crusted with old salt;
No longer were we detours forced to make;

White was the light, and green and blue the lake;
Nature seemed perfect, almost without a fault;
Clouds percolated through the sky's blue vault;
And trees showed browns and purples in the wake

Of the smoky tones that tinged their leafless arms;
Trees lay like symbols of the plaything green
That soon would ornament the playful scene
With blossoms flung like playtime's timeless charms

Onto this strident Nature, stretching far
To an illuminant edge, to where you are.

Your Dress

I am almost sick with your beauty
And the way that it pervades
My images, in lights or greys,
Or darks or blacks or shades;

You stand, almost palpable,
In the cinema of my mind;
The blessed colour that you wear
Is strong and soft, designed,

As if by a sorcerer's plot,
To enfold you entire;
Infinite infinities
It weaves from my desire

And will till veils of death
Descend to close my eyes
And the blessed colour of your dress
Fades into stars and skies.

Homage to *Swan Lake*

The endless road that leads to Art
Cannot be hailed as long or drear
Although its path is paved with fear;
Nor must it be stressed as long or far
If love be stressed as being near;

Countless seem murders of the soul
When, in Ego, one seeks a way
To the ultimate, infinite, intimate goal
Of sense, mind, and fantasy fused to a whole
Where nothing is needed that's left to say;

But, in a heartland place, there is a truth
That we are human and cannot run away
From humanness, and yet will *not* create
(Unlike our gods and goddesses) a Great
Conundrum where our cruelty holds sway;

It's in that heartland place we find our heart,
And sensate union find in sensate art.

Dancing for You

Why am I living, breathing, *dancing* for you mentally?
Because your inspiration breathes itself out all over me,
And the here where you are, and the here where I am,
Till emphatic growth nurtures my inward-felt minuets,
My arms to shake in a galliard *amour*, my mind
To jolt in frenzied seconds, line to line, faster
Than men can breathe, or women adjust their thoughts,
And on into a Romeo dance of longing
And down into a Hamlet dance of doubting
And off into a tremolo dance of a hand-and-fist
Shaking of dolors from a dream-enhanced shade,
Fitted, fretted, and furred with imaginative laces
And pearls, carbonated into a solid endearment,
A wall, a bravura pas de deux with you.

No Place Out There

A nightlife that is free of noise and beer
Is almost better than what I have right here
So long as you refuse to let me hold
You until the dawn light spreads its gold;

How ecstatic would be the din of an open bar,
The smell of rum, the swirl of a cigarette's smoke,
Compared to the smell of nothingness in my room
And the static curl of a silent blanket's cloak!

Thou hast no place out there, and nor have I;
Thee do I want, thine eyes in tune with mine,
Thy hair lying unflexed over thine eye,
Thy mouth a foretaste of a real Divine;

Oh, meet me, O my glory, my infatuate,
My feminine mounted on a downtrod potentate.

A Slight, Immaculate Touch

How I shall scream if I should part from thee!
Nowhere can Hell more bitter be than when
A slight, immaculate touch becomes a yen
For more than capacitance full and folly-free

To hold you to express, with arms, not verse,
My full attention to your torso, round
And slim, yet slightly and yet tightly wound
Like a coil ready to move, perhaps perverse;

O thou art Heaven unto a one like me
Who sighs and sees and sobs yet dares not speak
Of how this Earth without you would be bleak
To a master-point beseeching calumny;

Never were words, extreme as these might seem,
Framework for such a paintwork of a dream.

A Special Gift

I saw a film in which a lovely teen,
Who watched the heavens through her telescope,
Was given, by a boyfriend buoyed with hope,
A special gift that he had somehow seen

To be available: the naming of a star
After a special person, here, his friend;
Her smile of happiness would surely portend,
For him, a sort of ever-open bar

Of satisfied reciprocationality;
For, when she would die, the star would still shine on,
A star in the astronomic Pantheon
Of women worshipped for their empathy,

Their solaced pinings, their manifest desires,
Their longings for mementos forged from fires.

How Lightly the Light Sits ...

O my beloved monster, clean and pure!
How lightly the light sits on thy turmoiled head,
Flecking to gold the subtly coloured red
That hides in the browns of your hairline so demure!

I want to hold your head, to feel the skull
That hides your wonderful brain, to feel the tressed
Bewitchment of the individual hairs that pressed,
In repressured contact, against the pull

Or push of my hand, and equilibrium physical
Redolent of how the world plays out out there,
Whether we're talking of planets or of hair,
Every movement a cosmological miracle;

And yet such thoughts might hapless or hopeless be
To girls who'll never know the Mind of Thee.

Responses to You

To thee I plead my consciousness's cause;
To thee do I address these high-strung lines;
To thee I ask an occasional pause
So strong are my breath-beats' inner laws,
Responses to you as facts of Love's designs;

Thou art impossible, a merciless event
Of flesh and bone and blood and brain
Whose mind was surely from Olympus sent
To quite eradicate all good intent
Of mine, not to succumb once more, again,

To the tantalizing flow of a woman's dress,
To a smile promising Arcadias of content,
To a subtle laugh and finger's subtle stress
On a tabletop as promise of redress
For over-loving of which I now repent.

Unheralded

A slow and dreadful sickness can take root
When what one wants is real, instead of art;
Beauty can oust time's onslaughts, but cannot
Replace the beauty of a bodied heart

Yearned for and sought along a lifetime's years,
But only found, one day, in an unexpected place,
At an unexpected time, when sudden, silent, tears
Announced, unheralded, the advent of a grace

Undreamed of, far too far from fantasy,
The arrival of a movement, a dress, a face,
That spread an entrancement like epiphany,
An understanding that someone *can* replace

All dreams, all memories, all otherness
With unencumbered promise of redress.

Desisting

Up a mid-March slope of snow
The hesitating cars do go
As I these verses pen to Thee
But where they'll lead I do not know—

Will they down-skitter like a car
Whose driving cannot take it far
Because it slithers in the snow
Leaving a track way like a scar?

Will they urge up, with snort or boost,
Clattering up till they rule the roost
Of that snowy slope and intricate ice,
Or will they sink back as if all was lost?

O dangerous link between them and Thee,
I know that these verses are not, well, "free,"
But I also know that I cannot desist
From writing them, for they write me.

Dating

They sense the incoherence of my wits,
Do my "dates," a word I understand no more;
When slow I should move, I talk so fast, I bore;
And when fast I should move, I go in starts and fits;

When I should be there, smiling, in readiness
An infinite courtesy round them to display,
A sudden thought can push it quite away,
If I think of your charm and of your loveliness;

And when I should be bold—a goodnight kiss
Perhaps?—instead I furnish out a hand
For a neutral handshake, tactful, bleak, and bland,
While I think of your fingers and their promised bliss;

Oh, I should be destroyed; so stuck am I
In a quagmire of your making, I could cry.

Differential Threshold

Is this too true and timely to be borne?
Over and again have I Thee hugged,
Neutrally, eloquent, restrained, but warm;
Into the air between us pressed can swarm
Thoughts that the air itself has shrugged
Away as hope, not possibility;

But now I have felt Thy hand's simplicity;
Thou hast lent fervour to the lonely part
Played in previous holdings by a Thee
Powerful in resistance to the struggling me
Who strove to print the imprint of his heart
Upon the pure mind of Thy complicity;

And now the pure line of Thy woman's dominance
Has outed itself from Thy recalcitrance.

April

Animal

Down on my hands and knees I go
In sunshine, rainstorm, wind, and snow,
An animal by the gorgeous Thee
Whom I *so* much want to be nice to me;

I'll gambol and frolic for Thee all day,
Wash all the dishes and put them away,
Scramble around with a vacuum and mop,
Dustification of bookshelves to stop;

I'll put out the lights and lock up the door;
You'll never put garbage out no more;
I'll iron your blouses and always have coins
To wash and to dry what begirdeth your loins;

Oh what a house-husband I would be
If you'd only allow me to worship Thee.

I Cannot Charm Thee

I cannot charm thee; thou art too precipitous
In insight, too amalgamate in thoroughness
To be fooled by a set of smarmy phrases
That only make you think, "Oh, go to blazes …"
So charm, off into the toilet it must go.

I cannot boast or boost myself to thee;
It irritates you far too much to see
My progress when we're both so well aware
That many more years than you I have to spare,
And therefore know, well, more than you *could* know;

I cannot pretend to have a strength I don't;
I am, perhaps, less sociable than you'd want;
I'm out of fashion in this wireless age;
A tremor in my arms, I can't assuage;
And all of these are right, because they're so.

On and On …

You are not perfect like a polygon
Regular in angles and in sides;
You carve no image like Pygmalion,
A statue that a perfect goddess hides;
You are not smooth like Lake Opinicon
On a sunny day when quietness washes its rocks;
You are not deep as is the Amazon
Whose endless rain its forestland restocks;
You're not so young as was Endymion,
The Greek perfection of a virile boy;
You lack the symmetry of the Parthenon,
A place where warriors deploy;
But all your imperfections are for me
Symbols divine of your humanity.

Words

Words do not move, nor make the past to move;
Static they are, mere equilibria,
Making what's thought on that we wish to prove
To a fixed force, encyclopaedia;

Words cannot hide a heartbeat like a frown,
Nor can they goldenize when silver's hard;
Words that attempt to levitate go down
And words that seem pure are all too often scarred;

Words are quiet challenges of prose and sounds,
Discord abounds where union was before;
They bolster arguments on shaky grounds,
And turn the tables till they stand no more;

And all of this is wet-nurse for your fears
That I might feed you words for years and years.

Mental

Your slenderness I freely countenance,
And count the golden inches round your waist;
But mental that is, all mental, maintenance
Of frivolous fantasies I've always placed

On your being a Being romantically viewed
And yet observed too factually when you're real;
Harried, I scurry across an interlude
Between my wondering if you might conceal

Relief instead of sadness when you leave,
And if you try to hide, under your outdoor hood,
A silent sadness when you here arrive,
Because you think I've never understood

That what you want in me is more a friend
Than one who awaits the day when you'll unbend.

Verbal

When every little thing I've done or said
Gets exploded to a Sun or Moon instead
Because whatever I say to you, or do,
Is multiplied in my mind by thoughts of you

To inordinate in importance's rank,
The reason is as follows—I'll be frank—
My skirting round your sensitivities
Are games I play with my proclivities

To overpower you with the things I say.
So, I must cache my meanings, move away
From being explicit on what I most desire,
And muzzle myself to hide my secret fire,

Until the air between us breathes as free
As if nothing whatever, at all, bound you to me.

What I'll Give

Below, my darling, is what I want to give;
Let Waiting go and hang its weary head;
I want to show you what it means to live
In art and intellect, where men have spread

Their riches across the widest libraries,
Where knights who rescue damsels ride for real,
And silly cavorting in quiet sanctuaries
Seem so alive that you can really feel

You're part of a war, with human jokes for arms,
Against the pallid structures of dead kings,
And you can fight, wielding your woman's charms,
To woo the world away from war-like things;

And all of this will be my sublimation,
And none of this to you be degradation.

What I Want

I have astonished myself at how revealing
The thought, that I might humble myself to you,
Is of my desperation for a healing
That you can give me for disjunctions due

To wounds incurred in the battery of my life;
You do remind me of them, but also, besides
Revivication of past loss and strife,
You offer hope that there still stays and bides,

In you, in me, in both of us, a chance
For the past to go and the present made to stay;
Abasement (that I do not view askance)
Bids me to kneel, as if about to pray,

At your knee; but the truth is, what I think I want
You either do not want to give, or can't.

Springtime's Breath

Finer is beauty never to be found
Than when the psyche meets, on solid ground,
Those liquefying forces lying in wait
For April's tautest winds to generate
Youngness and greenness on every tree and bush,
And the rightness of Spring to re-fire all the "crush"
I've had for you since that memorable day
When your Autumn walk threw Springtime in my way.

Wonderful

A dusky orange starts to merge
Its colours with the yellow-greens;
Spring seems to stand upon a verge
Of forecasting Autumnal scenes;

But now the dark rain and rainy wind
Have nothing of Winter's fate attached;
All sustenance and nurtures find
Ordered outgrowth and newlings hatched;

Nothing of Autumn's dark is here;
The air is filled with spurt and fire;
The sky is concave arbour clear;
The animals, arbiters of desire;

And I see Thee, sombre and real,
Ready *Thy* wonders to reveal.

Oh God, It's Only Saturday

Oh God, it's only Saturday; three days
Must slide and slip and lapse until it's three
On a Tuesday afternoon, when you are free
To visit me, and I your grace to praise;

But the April sky is already veiling over
With dusk-enshrouded clouds waiting to storm
And flash the night in lightning's uniform
Before the next day's dawn begins to hover;

And will the raindrops then eradicate
Those midges multifarious born by Nature
And trapped in the Springtime's greening imprimatur?
Or will they stay to buzz and irritate

You, should you step into their midst outside,
Then run back in to find a place to hide?

Eventually

Here is my sanctum empty; you have gone
To where few golden suns have ever shone
Upon you in the way that they do here;
Here, revelation-sunshine near devout
Sheds down its gold upon the musing you,
As if a luminary were to cast about
Your perfect imperfections to construe.

Eventually will that light-plume light upon
The worth of Thee, O woman-paragon;
Stop; stand; cease; still; 'tis clear
That all incendiary motioning must flout
The respectful silence you are overdue;
See, through the windows, how the moon's come out
To flood, with its springtime strength, *your* silence too.

Grammar Lesson

Is evening a time to work, or play?
Neither; they're both the same; the term "and/or"
Is more descriptive of the way my mind
Tangles, all at once, with the metaphor

That, in entangling raucous talk with yours,
I tangle, with a purely imagined hand,
Your hair, whose lustre fills my eager heart,
And carried me, once, to an indescribable land

Where the deepest entanglement of my erstwhile life
Was undermined, and dispossessed of power,
By you; it's replaced by a stronger love for Thee,
In which I've tangled that treacherous pronoun "our"

Into a fusion-reference to "Thine,"
To which I've affixed, with trepidation, "mine."

May

When the Fog Lifts

When the fog lifts, a staggering climb of green
Emerges from the growing springtime hill;
Spatters of copper beech are interspersed
Between the veridians and emeralds
And evergreens, etched as they are in splatted
Colouring between the houses' tile-roofs;
Two hours ago, the grey was absolute,
A lucent grey that reached my balcony,
So close was it to my windows, a moistured grey
With nothing beyond, or what only could be guessed at;
But the grey has lifted, the green is singing again,
The sky has stripes of blue, and an inner song
Clutters my thought-streams when I try to think
Of all the things I want and cannot have.

Your Presence

A great and glowing presence
Seem you from far away;
From burdens of sadness within me
I veer where your presence holds sway;
And a thousand birds up-fly
Like battalions in the sky;

I sit on the edge of my chair
But my mind is filled by you;
Vicious are sadness's sounds
Although they all feel true;
So I run to where, in space,
Your presence holds its place;

And all my sadness whirrs
And dissipates into the night;
Into the emptiness I stir
New venturings of delight;
Oh, how I venerate
Your glowing presence great!

The Barrier

Looking out the window at the beauty of the landscape
I know there is a barrier, the window glass between;
Looking through the doorway as you walk beyond its threshold,
I know there is a barrier, but a barrier unseen;

Looking at you walking and exiting my doorway,
Sometimes I think to saunter behind, then embrace,
Ardent, your torso in the tenderest of arm holds,
But know that you would view that as improper and unkind;

So the barrier continues, you keep moving on away;
A Rubicon it constitutes, keeping us always two;
If cross I did, you'd feel I'd exerted control;
Control is what you want in order to feel you;

So on rolls the Rubicon, barrier unlifted;
Onwards go you with your hands-on controls;
Stagnant, stand I as you exit through my doorway;
Onwards the stalemating Rubicon rolls.

Night Begins

Hints of purple veil the waters
As Night begins to fold
The evening in its cloudy arms
Until, behind its cloudy charms,
The hidden sun burns gold;

Hints of longing veil my feelings,
And sadness you're not in sight;
I cannot see your cloudy arms
Or marvel at their cloudy charms;
All I can do is write.

A Generative Mind

Although it looks like steam, it need not be;
Cold air, on a springtime lake-top, turns to mist
And sends into higher air white moving clouds
That fringe the frigid lake-top like a sea;

Thus does the cold I've reluctantly shown to you
Simmer to send new condensations out,
From the flat unwavering surface of my mind,
That help to germinate new rhymes I've grown for you;

My rhymings, my sonnets, attempts at sonic grace,
Are softened sounds that try to warm the cold
Of the nothingness you have forced upon my thoughts;
If it feels like heat, it is; your place

Is to let me breathe a growing warmth upon
Your moon-like soul to burgeon it to sun.

Reading

I am enforced into blah, do-nothing postures;
I sprawl and lounge in my chair when I judge that my reading
Has reached a good stop-point when, satiated, I
Do not care to read on about mating and breeding,
Or frolic with romance in a dreamed-up pasture,
Because remorseless Time is going by,
And I fear that my urges to hold you might wither and die.

This is untrammelled lockdown of my dreams;
It's so unfair, unreasonableness blended
From frumpiness and frown, stirred to a brew;
Normalcy has been riddled and extended
Beyond a moderate edge into extremes;
Can never a short embrace be seen by you
As something to like, something you want to do?

This poem stands on the borderland of Hell;
I wrote it down by springing from the chair
Where I was idling, spent from a lengthy book
Persuading me that I was an animal's heir;
For example, this very verse is playtime well
Extended into age; whenever I praise your look,
I merely show how long my boyhood took.

Treetops

The treetops show their inner skeletons,
Sudden glimpses of tough extensive trunks
Beneath the topsy-turvy of the green;
Faint, thin, and fragile under the wash
Of green-touch seems their pencilaceous bulk,
Anchors of visual white in a leafy sea.

And so I see thee when it is we meet;
Anchored within your gorgeosities
Are sudden alarming moments unveneered
When vulnerabilities within your mind
Are suddenly glimpsed, then all but disappear
Beneath an overlay of sun-glazed clarity;

A visual veracity marks the hill,
And human truth is symbol of Thee still.

Each Night that Dawns

Each night that dawns with dew lit evening
Seems to ensconce all rigours, all constraints;
The night is scattered while the moon
A moonlight's mist on the rugged hilltops paints;

I wait for night to dawn and come and go,
So that the morning will adorn new day;
And that will bring me closer to the dawn
When you will cease to stay away, away;

There is no crepuscule devoid of day,
No gloaming to perpetuate the night;
Incessancies of changes chain the hours
With coruscations to the maverick light

That fills the morning where I wait to see
The clouds lift up and you alongside me.

Blossoms

One tree, befilled with blossoms, bloomed
In a merciless, but proud, aloneness there
On the springtime hillside; all alone in white,
Its colours combed and groomed the smiling air;

You are, for me, the only bloom;
You semi-castigate your sisters in
The mills of feminine humanity
Wherein the promptings of pure Art begin;

And only fragments of my looking
Pull me to others, a fanfare here or there
Of finest trilliums woven on the ground;
Your dominance, though, determines me to swear

That we, arm in reluctant arm, and side by side,
Ensure that your blossoming does not peak and then subside.

Fireworks, Again

All these fired-up fireworks feel so false,
Lights going up and then exgurgitating;
Life has no meaning if it goes not up,
And artificial life is just frustrating;

You find yourself, as I do, all in doubt,
Staring, with questioning thoughts asunder,
At life, and at how it plods its weary way
Along what ought to be a road of wonder,

But instead is a thorny, bitter-paved path
Partitioned with branches of the unachieved,
Scored by the brambles of incompetence,
Tarnished by promises unbelieved;

You look, as I do, directionless, here and there,
Peering for perfections everywhere.

Your Hair

Th' impassioned beauty of your mind doth underlie
The shining beauty of your quasi-russet hair;
Each strand is a model of your vincibility;
Each rippled fold, as it riffles through and about the air,
Sings tunefully about the suitability
Of your hair's being a symbol of your mutability,
Folding and changing, although it cannot assert just why;

I sigh as you stand there; I do not, but I want to, stretch out my hand
To pat and pamper the beauty that is your shining hair;
I want to hold it as gently as if it were alive,
And mollify it with whispered suggestions to stay right there,
And allow me to mould its foldings, as though it could never thrive
As a wiriness fixed, but, instead, was straining to strive,
To put, in your mind, a changeable softness you *did* understand.

Fires of Artifice

Now, suddenly, the fireworks have grown quiet;
A silence stretches down beneath the sky
That, darkening, fills full an empty void,
While the silence seems a sound about to die;

I look as if I were a counterweight
To the all-seeing cosmos of the air;
I shudder in abrogation of my sight
And cancel out the dinnings of my ear;

Static, a photograph I seem, etched as if
A creature from a foreign-born dimension
Had snapped me in non-motion at a time
When I can find no freedom from my tension;

And you, instead of smiling at these stills,
Sigh and search on for what your need fulfils.

June

Her Arms

The summer is here and now I see her arms;
Shielded they were in winter by her clothes,
Or knitted jerseys, or insignia
That covered her skin and shielded her from harms;

So right for me are her arms, I want to swoon,
But cannot let my maleness e'er disclose
That such an impassioned egomania
Should ever make me whiten and fall down;

So I don't faint; I ogle her arms, am envious
Of how they lie beside her in repose
While just her hands silently weave an aria
Of movement and longing and meaning, but abstemious;

Such a portrait, such still life, such waiting,
Seem on her arms beatitudes to impose,
While, lucent with latent melancholia,
I try to counter any anticipating

Of favours from those smooth and marvelous arms;
I sigh, because my wanting will not wane; it grows;
I do not want my memorabilia,
My fantasies of her, to lose their charms.

I Don't Understand Myself

I am too immoderate for modesty
To blur its weary way into my open self
Unless, of course, some higher Power awaits, and plots
For will, with *its* power, to come and overwhelm
Immoderation, pulverizing to
Abasement what had been proud, but then was not,
As if to purge immoderation from my soul.

But, should that Power's existence be in question,
Then must immoderation seem more normal,
Then must my poorish Ego flex for a fight;
It should be seen as preparation-world
For a prouder world in me, where I can prove
That I, no favourite of the gods, deserve
At least one lover more to round my life.

Wanting

A golden bleach betrays your ardour'd eyes;
How can I stand, as you stand, unbereft
Of a wanting to fuse our eyes until the rise
Of a wanton sun cajoles what wants are left
Into activity, or compromise?

Let there be stand-down to this standing off;
Let there be drift from black-and-white to grey;
Let there be lurching from your backing off;
Let a breach of breath, like a breaking day
That pours its greyness on the sloughing off

Of an archipelago from a sea-girt land,
Breathe its out-stopped air to mould and soften
The maddening non-movement of your hand,
Letting me dream you are for real more often.

The Miracle of Life

The huge and monstrous miracle called Life
Straddled, like a burden, all that time
I spent dissecting books to find out if
The life that I had blithely thought was "mine"
Was actually owned by a "gene-pool," serpentine
Sometimes, but mostly stuck and stiff.

How stupid to hope I'd join your genes to mine!
How ridiculous it was to fantasize
I'd hold your arms as if they were divine
Intoxicants that I could ecstatize
And, trance-like, thus immortalize
Their proof that an Intelligent Design,

That of a Goddess-Grace, had had them made
For one like me to hymn and accolade!

Resistance Level?

This is my century of verse to Thee
And I am too faint to contemplate their rhymes;
They stand like bursts of teardrops broken free
From the stifling weight of stifling waiting times;

I hear Thee speak, or see Thee start to walk,
Or spy on the motions of Thy moving knees,
Or sense, reverberating through our talk,
Quixotics in our haltered repartees,

Or watch how the love you ladle on your sounds
Seems to impart, to my over-eager ear,
Jungle enhancements of what is out of bounds
As if you brought your temptingness so near

That what had been far now seemed much more direct:
But where, oh, where am I in your intellect?

Spontaneous Generation

Loveliness rivets you against the sunset;
Against the high sky's glow of yellow-red
Stands the dark outline of your silhouette
And faintly are seen the features of your head;

Your hair falls to shoulders whose fairness brings a thrill
Of chiaroscuro to its dark contact,
While hidden in shadow, a gleam of an eye-gleam still
Renews my hope that you'll feel moved to act

To move and touch me lightly with your hand,
Or spread, across the air, a smile to say
That I am entitled to think, you understand
Why my hope to have you has not yet gone away

And never will, so long as I feel you hide
An instinct to move to join me to stand at my side.

July

Fireworks Yet Again

Setting the fireworks off before the night
Has fully fallen tarnishes their light
And their dusty twinklings seem to lose their might;

Writing these lines to you before I've known
The gilded comfort of being with you alone
Lends to their reality an unreal overtone.

Download

Now logic has swungen down and taken away
A moment's surrender that did not seem like play,
So soon and swooning it was, and genuine;

And logic now will build around you walls
Ever so silent, and ever so secret, till falls
A holy darkness around you, undivine.

I'll Want to Know

I know the wrenching misery of madness
And how it must be kept at bay, away;
But if you go, I'll want to know
What it was I failed to say;

I know the infinite hurling of remorse
But cannot feel I've ever done you wrong
But if you go, I'll want to know
If you were acting all along;

I know the kicking of oneself with gall
At a stumbled innuendo's stumbled gaffe;
But if you go, I'll want to know
If you ever hid an urge to laugh;

But if you stay, I'll know there is no myth
That's powerful enough to praise you with.

Relief

Poetry is the single most relief;
Its light slides slowly up the greenest hill
And fertilizes its top with honey'd dew;
It is a hold-keep for one's disbelief
And for those longings that one dares not view
As fillable in a world that crowds us still
With blockages and moral overkill.

Why hast Thou *not* deserted me now, my muse?
Why is my pen still straggling along
The lines of this contoured page, and why am I
Still sitting, controlled by fuming words and brews
Inviolate, with growth infused, and why
Am I still grappling with fits of song
Whose bursts astringent are, and yet are strong?

You

I saw a thunder overtake a sky
That on that morning free of cloud had been,
And knew I had to talk to you of why
I fear riposte will overtake our clean

Unsullied discourse free of harm;
My admiration is not, as I once wrote
To someone else, "cold as my brain," but warm
It is with love that weaves an antidote

Against all casual name-calls or despites;
No quarrel should ever uncorrected be,
For fear a festering might disease the nights
And days when, even though you're not with me,

I think of you as the warm and lovely child
Who me to humankind hath reconciled.

August

Shoreline

The first boat and the first faint morning sprawl
Of the lakeside's far and opposite shore appear;
The sunlight starts to lift and rise and fall
As the mists lift and the birds begin to call;
And I wait for Thee, Thy voice, Thy smile, Thy walk,
And the fumbled near-depravity of my talk;

How like a dawn light morning weaves Thy grace
Across the hall and doorways waiting here!
I'm almost breathless when you grace this place,
Lending appropriate logic to my space,
So full and cramped with seriousness it is,
So aching for your woman's levities!

The first faint sprawl of shore has disappeared;
The boat has gone; but You remain revered.

The Streamline

Sometimes there bursts, an unplanned cannon-shot,
From my mind, an irresistible intent
To blaze you forcefully, in verses that I dare not
Bridle, informing all the readers who read me
What an illustrious gemling I have caught,
Coiled in a jewel-box deep in me inside,
Whose beauty is so strong and undefied
That nothing in Heaven or Earth will dare impede me.

My chest, none too barreled, my whimpery throat,
My somewhat arthritic, yet pen-holding, hand
Are competing as if to grapple the boat
That she is propelling along a stream,
Keeping it level, aloft and afloat,
In a new moon, a feminine Galahad,
Silvern, in wondrous armour clad,
A physical knight in my life-saving dream.

The Hours Fall By

Slowly the hours fall by, like snow on a lateral path;
Whatever minutes go by when you are not here, I fill
With trajectoried wond'rings as to whether the aftermath
Of all our talks will be fantasizing meanderings till,

Well, *nothing* strikes, fruitless, on a gong; or, at best,
A bell will toll to call the fledglings of the night
To a slumber within a cold and cathedralic nest;
Or whether a sudden filling, a *ful*filling of light

That shines, with a fit and a sombre and a true reality,
Upon my side of our talks, will burst into suddenly being,
And I can stand by you for more than this stark temporality
Of "now and again" and instead entertain a future where seeing

You every day, will scatter a major dust of You
Over times I not only want to see you, but actually do.

September

How Late the Dawn Is

How late the dawn is when September starts ...
Dawn, when a whole half-world smiles up
At the waiting sun, begins to lighten here
In June at 5 a.m.; but now, as September
Begins her somewhat weary lurch to winter,
There is, at 6 a.m., just minor light
Beginning to rim the treed horizon's tops;
And house lights peer into the dark, and scarce
Is any hum or roar of a bus or train
Beginning its round; more light must wait
For later, just as I
Must wait and wait until the dark's repaired.

The Marvelous and Mystical and Magical

How marvelous and mystical and magical,
How wondrous bordering on miracle,
Are the ecstatic blazonries you display
On storm or winter night or summer day;

And I just stare, aghast
At the ghosts of Romance Past,
And at how the wafts of your waving hair
Make them vanish to who knows where.

October

Portrait

I peer through a wall of falling rain
At a scudding sky and at reddening hills
Where the Fall is branding her leaves again
With the endless colours her bounty spills;

I see you across a table's space,
Your guard is down and you curl your knees
Beneath your body, while over your face
Spills a smile in response to my unspoken pleas

To stay like that, an image of pleasure,
A moment captured, like leaves in the Fall,
As Nature's beauteous bountiful treasure,
With you as her treasure most lovely of all;

And, as Fall breathes her beauty across this land,
Yours is a bounty I newly understand.

It Is You …

You have entranced me so much, it is you
Who has really written all this; you fed
All the thoughts you conceived in my mind, and your words
Enchantingly embraced the moving air
So movingly, I was laid low
Numbed by the miracle of your being there.

And now may you give, to your wide-world work,
The sense of renewal you gave to me;
Let your fine mind, as it bends to a book,
Entrance to effulgence whatever may flow
In those rivers of thought that enliven that mind;
May you enhance it to widening Truth,
Magicalized by the power of your youth,
And the new understanding you poured into me.

Fade Out

Time is passing and thy distant conquests fade;
The timely havocs and the happy marks they made
Upon my eager upward-stretching mind cascade
Into a past that's lastingly displayed;

For, even though elsewhere thou goest away
And maybe no rival should ever know the sway
And pull that burnished my every breathing day,
That Past in my present mind will stay and stay.